Who Says You Have To Grow Up

Zoe Matthews

BookLeaf Publishing

India | USA | UK

Presentation by *BookLeaf Publishing*

Web: www.bookleafpub.com

E-mail: info@bookleafpub.com

ISBN : 9789357448635

First edition 2021

DEDICATION

To my mother, Haylee

For giving me a childhood to remember

To my students, especially 11Bio1

For sharing the joys of their own childhoods

ACKNOWLEDGEMENT

Thank you to my family for encouraging my love of reading, to Oliver for supporting me in everything I do, and to Kirstyn for pushing me to take the step into poetry.

PREFACE

Life is full of ups and downs, something we now know better than ever. Many of us have spent much of the pandemic wishing for the past, something we saw as a much simpler time. The irony is as children, we longed for the future, to be grown up, to do all the things that "grown ups" do. This collection of poems is reminiscent of childhood memories and the childlike wonder we've all experienced. Each poem is titled with the "grown ups" version, a reminder that everything we do now is not all that far off from our childhoods, that even in all this chaos, we are still children at heart.

The Blind Date

Who would have thought it
A bond as strong as this
Brought together by fate
Sharing smiles of pure bliss

A warmth grows within
A love as strong as steel
Every moment shared
Together for every meal

Strangers now inseparable
No need to even chase
Now the best of friends
Pulled into your embrace

Always soft to the touch
Their hand held tight in yours
Slowly getting dirty now
Too many adventures outdoors

With you they stay
For you will always care
As they watch you grow
Your little teddy bear

Playing with Food

Sitting up in the highchair
For lunch you have yogurt and pear
First time controlling the spoon
Only little, maybe it was too soon
Now it is all through your hair

The Butterfly

A small girl races
Through the deep green forest trees
Chasing butterflies
Light makes her eyes sparkle as she gazes up at
the one she chases
Climbing over fallen stumps and small
creatures' homes
Her arms are spread out, pretending she is a bird,
fairy and butterfly all at once
Her only focus is the little white butterfly above
her head
Childlike wonder pulls her spirits up higher as
the butterfly goes higher
Her laughs floating on the wind, the butterfly
gently follows
The forest opens into a clearing full of bright
yellow daisies

Fancy Water

Today is the day
The day mum lets you have it
Finally, the fancy water!
You open the fridge and grab it

Balancing the bottle while you walk
Being careful as you hold it
Too big for your little hands
But you really want to try it

Passing it to mum at the bench
She places the green cup next to it
Undoing the lid, it lets out a hiss
Slowly into the cup she pours it

Half full, she passes you the cup
You look in to check you got it
The fizzing present but faint
Bubbles float up from within it

You raise the cup and take a sip
Bubbles popping as you drink it
Always wanting, but now seems odd
Looking at mum "what is it?"

She looks at you with a loving smile
"Sound out the letters, you know it"
One word, not fancy water
Lemonade! That's i

Do It Yourself

Bright pots of colour
Waiting to be used in art
What will you create?

Dip in your fingers
Make them extra colourful
Spread on white canvas

Drag them up and down
Colours mixing together
A shape slowly forms

Yellow, blue, green too
A big bright sun, spikey grass
The flowers come last

The Unwelcome Guest

They came into your world
Without even a warning
You had a great life
Up until this morning

It started well
Until mum felt funny
Dad packed the car
Said "it's okay, honey"

Now grandma is here
She makes you pancakes
You play some games
With lots of snack breaks

It's time for bed
Quick go pee
A fun day had
But where could they be?

The sun comes up
They're still not here
Could they just leave you?
You start to fear

Nothing could be more important than you
A knock at the door signals their return
Still don't know why
But you're about to learn

You follow them to the lounge
They prop you up in a chair
Mum holds something to you
A baby? No thanks. Don't want to share

They were your parents first
This is merely a stranger
No longer the only child
Your attention now in danger

Desires of the Heart

Many an adventure to be had
Anywhere you could ever want to go
Keep the creativity high, excitement building up
Exaggerating the world to make it your own

Be whoever you want to be
Elves and fairies out in the garden
Lead the princess to safety, slay the dragon
Invisibility, flight, super strength and speed
Enchantments and spells from an ancient wizard
Vampires and werewolves fighting it out
Explore the depths of outer space, from your bed

Making Gold

Wiggle. Wobble. Pop
A little tooth now in hand
Rushing to show mum

Put it in a cup
Make sure it is nice and clean
Trade the tooth for gold

Now that it is dry
Deciding where to store it
What would be safest?

Under your pillow?
What if it falls on the floor!
How about a glass?

Safely in the glass
Up on the bedside table
Excitement bubbling

When will she arrive?
What could you spend the gold on?
So many options

Trying to stay up

Wanting to see her fly in
Her wings fluttering

Waking up at dawn
The sun rays guiding your gaze
Checking the safe place

No more little tooth
A gold coin now in its place
The Tooth Fairy came!

The Sneaky Snack

Grumble and moan
Looking down at your tummy
You rub above your belly button
Heading into the kitchen

Growl and rumble
Pulling open the pantry door
Gazing up to the top shelf
Spotting the special biscuit tin

Gurgle and stir
Desire takes over
You must get up there
Carefully placing small feet on boxes

Groan and whine
Your own personal rock climbing wall
Looking for the gaps to hold
The tin almost in reach

Grip and hold
Fingers graze the tin
Slowly pulling towards you
Trying not to fall back down

Gulp and smile
The tin wide open, biscuits in hand
So many options to choose
Shovel them in before you get caught

Who Wants a Nap?

The struggle is real
All you want to do is play
With dolls to dress, cars to drive, things to draw
And it was just about time to chase the cat
How can you do any of that if you're asleep?

Thrashing about as you're picked up
All you want to do is stay awake
Carried away from the toys and the fun
Placed in your bed, not wanting to sleep
The blanket wraps around you

What is this torture?
All you want to do is run
Babble on, must convince them you're not tired
Trying to wiggle, can you get the sheet off?
Like a snake it just gets tighter

Snug as a bug, tucked in tight
All you want to do is yawn
Your head sinks down
A warmth all around you
Trying to hold on but your eyes drift off

Rainy Days

Pitter Patter, Pitter Patter
The sound of rain against the glass
Pitter Patter, Pitter Patter
Droplets covering the grass

Excitement builds, rushing to mum
Begging "please can I go outside?"
Grabbing gumboots, coats and hats
Not waiting till it's dried

Spot the biggest puddle you can
Running full speed towards it
Laughter bubbling from within
Too close, can't stop, can't quit!

Splish Splash, Splish Splash
A spray of water as you tumble in
Splish Splash, Splish Splash
Wet as a dog with a massive grin

Starting New

The first day is always the hardest
Mum lays out your brand new uniform
Dad helps you tie your shoes
Says one day he will teach you how to do it

Walking through the big front gates
Each parent holds a hand
Nerves begin to grow
Not knowing what to expect

You make it to the classroom
Not wanting them to leave
Tears fill your eyes, then theirs too
One last embrace, you finally say goodbye

The hometime bell rings
A sound you are not yet used to
You see them waiting in the crowd
Before rushing over to hug them

They ask if you had fun
Holding up your drawing
Your name written in the corner
"Let's get home and put it on the fridge"

Building a Home

Pull the blankets from your bed
Inch the kitchen chairs against the lounge
Leave some space to make it big
Launch sheets and blankets in the air
Over the sides of couches and chairs
Working together, making it solid and strong

For now you have your very own castle
Only now you need to fill it
Remaining pillows thrown under
The castle is ready to play

Staying the Night

A sleepover is a joyous event
Binge watching movies is how it is spent
Pizza and lollies strewn over the floor
Staying awake till half past four
Aren't you glad you went

Daydreaming

Laying on the grass
Looking up at the sky
Thinking clouds are fluffy
White blobs just floating by

Watching the shapes
What animal can you make?
Maybe a sheep, a rabbit or a bear
Daydreaming, but still wide awake

A massive cloud appears
Exclaiming "it's a whale!"
A friend disagrees,
They think it's a snail

The bell rings loud
Quick, spot your last creature
Racing back to the classroom
Can't wait to tell the teacher

A Celebration

Rushing in the front door
Bag dumped on the kitchen floor
Calling hello to mum and dad
They ask about the day you had

As you head outside to play
Mum empties out your bag, all put away
Pulling out your lunch box
Hidden below, a paper with a little fox

Unfolding as she reads
An invitation proceeds
"You are invited…"
She knows you'll be delighted

The day draws near
Finding the perfect gift for a new year
Arriving at the party, asking mum to stay
Handing over the gift, "HAPPY BIRTHDAY"

Joining friends with a matching party hat
Face painting time, you go for the cat
Pass the parcel. Duck, duck, goose
Tired out. Quick! Grab some juice

From the games you take a break
Out now comes the birthday cake
Vanilla? Chocolate? You can only guess
Quickly in your mouth. Oh, what a mess!

Never Trust the Shadows

Never look under the bed
You don't know what you'll find
Maybe it will just be a sock
But maybe it is not

Never look under the bed
It is where the monsters live
How many are there?
Do you even want to know?

Never look under the bed
Not game enough for it to look back
Bright green eyes, maybe red
Piercing bright against the dark

Never look under the bed
Don't even dangle your feet
Who knows what could happen
What if you were pulled right in?

Never look under the bed
Even if you lost a toy
Keep your hand from the shadows
It is not worth the risk

How to be Cool

Summer comes, winter now long gone
The heat growing harder to avoid
Trying to cool off, but don't have a pool
Just wishing you could jump in the refreshing
void

The AC now blasting
Fans rotating on full speed
Ice block in hand, feeling a droplet on your leg
Can't tell if melting ice, or a sweat bead

Dad goes out to the shed
He tells you "meet me in the front yard"
Not sure what he has in store
Still fanning yourself with a christmas card

The hose now connected to the tap
What is the thing now on the end?
It is the trusty water sprinkler!
In this heat, it feels like a godsend

Turn the tap on high
Water rushing through the pipe and holes
An instant chill runs through your body
Jumping and splashing like little tadpoles

The Hidden Sparkle

Tipping a box out,
A little sparkle mixed in the pile.
Curiosity taking over, pushing everything off,
Wanting to know what secrets the box has to
share.
The shine now within reach,
Light reflecting back a rainbow of colours!
Thoughts racing, trying to work out what it
could be,
Memories filling your thoughts.
A marble, long separated from the rest,
The winner of games once played.
A happy smile forming,
Schoolyard enjoyment flooding back.
Held up to the light,
Glitter shimmering through!

Meeting in the Streets

Music plays across town
As the ice cream truck drives up and down
Everyone runs out into the streets
All wanting ice cream treats
No matter if you are in a suit or dressing gown

Curfew

Helmet in hand, half way out the door
Hearing mum's voice and her loving call
"Be safe. Have fun. Be home before dark"
Always the same, "I know" you call back
Stumbling over the hose, heading for the fence
There she is, your trusty steed
Waiting, ready, wanting to be ridden
Mere seconds and you're on the road
Gaining speed as you fly past parked cars
Reaching your friends house, everyone's there
Together you ride, all over town
Stomachs begin to grumble and stir
Cured only by piping hot chips from the corner
store
You eat at the park, bikes scatter the ground
The sun slowly setting, a chill slowly forming
Back in the seat, the group still together
One by one, friends turn down their street
Until you reach yours, right as the lights come
on

www.ingramcontent.com/pod-product-compliance
Lightning Source LLC
Chambersburg PA
CBHW070725160726
48003CB00006BA/2378